Truth Street:
A Hillsborough Poem

Truth Street:
A Hillsborough Poem

David Cain

Smokestack Books
1 Lake Terrace, Grewelthorpe, Ripon HG4 3BU
e-mail: info@smokestack-books.co.uk
www.smokestack-books.co.uk

ISBN 9781999674243

Smokestack Books
is represented
by Inpress Ltd

'April is the cruelest month, breeding
Lilacs out of the dead land, mixing
Memory and desire, stirring
Dull roots with spring rain.'
TS Eliot, *The Wasteland*

To the ninety-six people
who lost their lives
at Hillsborough in 1989
and for football fans
everywhere.

These poems are developed from evidence given at the Second Inquest into the Hillsborough Stadium Disaster. The inquest opened in Warrington on 31 March 2014, the jury heard 296 days of evidence. More than 500 witnesses were called and 4,000 pages of documents and hours of video evidence were shown.

On 6 April 2016, the nine jurors were sent out to consider their verdicts. These were formally given to the inquests on 26 April 2016.The jury returned a verdict of unlawful killing in respect of all 96 victims (by majority verdict of 7–2).

Transcripts of the proceedings and evidence produced during the hearings are published on the Hillsborough Inquests official website:

http://hillsboroughinquests.independent.gov.uk.

Contents

‘

The Afternoon

People were in a good mood

It wasn't just male fans.

There was men, women, children.

There was a lot of families there.

They were very happy.

Lots of people eating chips, milling around,

Going into the ground.

Looking forward to going to watch the football match.

A special match.

A big match.

A semi-final.

I remember seeing officers on horses

I have a habit of stroking them

Giving mints to them.

I bumped into a friend and we were just chatting.

There was a little wall

Where the blue outer gates are.

A stream goes under it.

I sat there reading my programme, mooching about.

Watching the world go by.

It was all happy.

It was a nice sunny day.

2.40pm

There were a lot of supporters standing around waiting.

It was a mass,

A mass of people in a relatively small area.

They were coming from Leppings Lane.

And heading down towards the turnstiles.

It was unusual.

At home matches, away matches

People are queuing up in two's

Taking turns to go through one after the other.

Little rows snaking out from turnstiles,

But there was just one massive throng of people.

A mad scramble

No queues.

Just a lot of people.

A solid mass of people waiting to get into the ground.

Chief Superintendent David Duckenfield looks at the monitor

I saw people were spilling off the pavement

We ordered the road to be closed.

I could see fans being pushed against the wall.

I was very concerned, because there were young people in amongst this.

The situation was becoming unmanageable.

'It's chuffing rammed.'

A mixture of screams

involuntary noises,

gasps , wheezes

noises of exasperation and desperation,

and the horrible thing was, some of this was tempered,

with what seemed like almost merriment

from people who were still joining the throng at the very, very back.

2.44pm

I was squashed in the middle of that throng.

Trying to get to the turnstiles.

I get the feeling they realised they'd lost control.

I remember one mountie in particular.

It is a very strong memory.

One particular mountie on a police horse

trapped right down at the far end against the turnstiles

as if he was actually splattered against the wall at the far end,

caught out by the throng milling around him and suddenly
hemming him in.

I remember him pushing past me as he tried to get his horse out.

I think he realised his horse was in danger of stampeding.

I was being crushed to death

You were that squashed with all of the people around you.

You were praying for there to be an elbow movement,

an arm movement,

So that you could move your diaphragm and take in a little bit of air.

The 20-footstep journey took 20 minutes.

It wasn't so much a decision

just a survival instinct,

to get through the turnstile,

worm and push and wriggle and duck and dive

and try to get to the front before the panic sets in.

I ended up face blank stuck against the brick wall

A bit like rubbing yourself against a piece of solid sandpaper.

horrible sharp

nothing nice or rounded or polished

just the sharp

stark

2.47pm

Someone open the gates

He was referring to opening of the exit gates.

I was quite shocked.

It was totally unprecedented.

It was something you just didn't do.

To open exit gates.

You lose control.

But he came back and said words with more urgency,

'I want the gates to be opened.

Open the gates.

If you don't open the gates, someone's going to get killed.'

I remember saying quite clearly,

'If people are going to die, I have no option but to open the gates.'

The sole thought was that I'd got to save lives.

I only thought about the room on the concourse.

If people outside those gates were in danger of dying,

or being crushed.

They would feel relief and comfort in the concourse.

I didn't consider any other consequences.

That is one of the biggest regrets of my life.

I did not foresee where fans would go

when they came in through the gates.

It just opened

It were like sand into an egg timer.

It was the strangest thing.

It just opened and stayed open.

I think it must have been sanctioned.

People realised it was a quicker way of getting in.

There was people just walking through.

Very calm, you know, no rushing or anything.

They walked through

like sand into an egg timer.

I wanted to buy a couple of programmes

While I was seeing to that, they gave me the slip.

There was a large London element, the London supporters' club,

and the girls were known as 'The London girls.'

So they would meet up with their friends.

There was boys and girls involved,

and having their old man around wasn't popular.

The girls went off down the tunnel.

I recognised a lad from Liverpool

Actually came out of the tunnel

the middle

the problem tunnel

actually came out of there and we bumped into each other

and he said,

'Don't go in there.

Don't go in there.

It's murder in there.'

He was coming out because it was so bad.

We decided we'd see if there was another way onto the terracing.

So we walked back out of the tunnel

and we spoke to a steward and asked the question,

'Is there another way to get into the pens without going through the tunnel?'

He pointed back down the tunnel and said,

'Just go back down there.'

2.59pm

This massive surge from behind came.

It was violent and sudden.

And sent us scuttling down towards the front of the pens.

I was pushed down the terracing.

It was coming from behind me on the left.

A river of people

suddenly entering the terracing from the centre tunnel.

Pushing the people that were already standing there forward.

The scene reminded me of pictures on television in the nature programmes.

Molten lava

Molten lava flowing down a hillside from an active volcano.

like a wave.

down towards the terrace.

Wave after wave coming in from behind you

there was no going

back.

It was unbearable

I have never felt anything like it in my life.

It was hard to breathe.

I wanted my big brother to help me.

I was scared and I was looking for him to try and resolve

the situation for me.

My main focus was trying to breathe.

It was a battle to try and stay on your feet.

Stay breathing.

It was just stay on your feet

stay breathing,

don't go down.

My father had his hands on the railings

I cradled him

trying to protect him from the pressure.

My dad turned around to face me,

And he had a look of just sheer terror on his face.

I could see that.

I just said to him that he would be okay.

From that point, it became worse, and I was really, really
concerned for my dad, for myself.

Then there was a sudden surge from the back.

I couldn't hang on any further with my hands,

And my arms buckled.

And I was twisted to the right-hand side, with my back to the
fencing

With bodies just pressed from all sides against me.

That is the last time I had my father alive.

There was like a silence

It was just an eerie sound.

It probably only lasted a second or two.

But it felt like a lot longer.

It's hard to describe the sound.

I've never heard the sound since.

As it seemed to settle, people started screaming and panicking.

It wasn't nice. It was people screaming, people crying all at the same time.

The noise is almost impossible to describe.

People screaming, people shouting for kids

People shouting to the pitch side for help.

It was so hot. The smell was terrible and lingered in the air.

Sweat. Heat. Vomit.

The smell is not something I have ever smelt before and I have never smelt it since.

Is it the smell of death?

I don't know.

We were in the same class in school

I hadn't seen him for quite a while, since we left school.

We ended up on the barrier together

It was a strange place to meet someone.

 We were both on the barrier, squashed up

He said to me, 'When's it going to stop?'

It was just getting worse and worse.

He was shouting out,

'Fucking hell. Fucking hell.'

There was nothing I could do for him .

He was bent very far forward over the barrier.

He looked around and his face was very, very red.

His eyes were very wide, distress and panic on his face.

'Help me. Get me back. Get me off this barrier.'

It was right across his hips and his stomach.

I was trying to pull him back, trying to pull him upright and

pull him away from the barrier.

It was no use.

There was that much pressure coming from the tunnel behind us.

I shouted, screamed for people to help.

And all these hands came over him from behind.

And started pulling him back off the barrier as best as they could.

Even given the distress that people were in themselves.

They were still doing everything they could to help others.

He was screaming his legs were trapped,

His legs were going to break.

He was in a great deal of distress.

I had hold of his arms

he was looking at me, and I was looking at him,

and we separated.

I couldn't hold onto his hand anymore.

My whole world was in that one pen at that moment.

I couldn't breathe

The girl next to me was shouting,

'Help me, help me.'

And the man in front was screaming about his legs being trapped.

He was just pinned against the barrier.

and he was shouting,

'Hold me up, hold me up'

So I put my arms underneath his armpits and tried to hold him up,

but then my legs got trapped

and then the last I remember is someone saying,

'The barrier's about to go'

I heard his knee crack.

We fell through the barrier

When the barrier collapsed, it went down, my legs were underneath and my body went over the top.

I found myself kneeling and scrambling on top of people

And the man I was trying to hold up was underneath me,

And I had my arms trapped under his armpits.

And somebody said to me, 'Let go of him, let go of him'

and I said, 'No, I'm holding him up'

and he said, 'Don't bother, mate,

He's dead

Open the gate

We didn't have a key to open it.

We hadn't had any instructions.

We turned and we tried to find out who's got a key.

We were saying to the sergeant,

'Who's got a key?

Who's got a key?

Can we open the gates?'

Some were just shouting,

'Open the gate,

open the gate'

and clawing at the fencing.

There was a man in front of me

He was virtually part of my body, my ribs.

I was like a rag doll.

I was really struggling.

The pressure was enormous,

It was squeezing it out of you.

I was losing consciousness.

I remember waking up very briefly,

somebody had got hold of me by my hair

literally pulling me up by my hair.

Somebody's arm was across my throat.

stopping me from breathing.

My feet weren't touching the floor.

I was literally hanging off this man's arm.

I was trying to ask him to move his arm because his arm was choking me.

I was pleading with him to move his arm, but he couldn't.

He was dead.

The police were treating it as a sort of pitch invasion

Trying to push people back into the pen.

I was shouting that people were dying, let people out,

they didn't respond.

They could hear us.

I produced my warrant card.

I thought if they realised I was a policeman

and I was saying that people are dying,

then they would respond.

I held it up in the air.

I said, 'Why wasn't they letting people out?

There's people dying in there.'

You murdering bastards

You Yorkshire pigs.

You murdering bastards.

3.05pm

A young man came from the perimeter track behind the goal and collapsed.

I remember seeing him hobbling from the back of the goal and collapsing on the pitch.

And gradually I think realisation dawned on them

It wasn't a pitch invasion.

It wasn't hooliganism.

There was something wrong.

The police then were trying to pull the people out of the pen

We used ourselves as ladders.

Sticking our knees through the railings

and telling people on the inside to use the knees as a step,

climb over the fence and use our bodies to climb down as a ladder.

I saw some police bashing the spikes down with their bare hands

I recall seeing a number of officers punching, kicking at the meshing

Police and fans alike

Pulling down the wire fencing immediately behind the goal in order to get people out.

It was very, very difficult.

I think it was very, very well made, the front of the fencing,

but in the situation that they were in,

they did keep going pulling at it with bare hands,

until they managed to pull the fencing away

to find a hole big enough to get people through.

Everything went peaceful

Everything turned white.

There was a police lady

and I felt her touching my face with her fingers

through the small holes on the fence

she had her fingers trying to prick me on the cheek saying,

'Hang on, you're strong, get through this',

and then things went white again

and the next thing I remember,

was being dragged along and out of the gate.

The call for a fleet of ambulances comes approximately 2 minutes and 40 seconds after the request for dogs

When the crowd eased back

People who had died

Because the pressure eased,

The bodies just fell back.

I grabbed the railing,

pulled myself up,

And the image that I'll never forget

Was of the boy behind me falling backwards.

We began to pull people out

Many of them appeared to be in a panic.

They was just rushing towards the open gate to try and get out.

One fan was in such distress that,

having got out of the pen himself,

he was trying to get back in to help others.

I remember that one.

He kept two or three times,

He kept trying to go back.

Should I go in?

I noticed a small gap

I thought

If I get in there,

I have a chance

I were looking at the gap and I thought,

Shouldn't I go in?

If you're going to do it, you've got to do it now,

because the longer you wait here,

the worse it's going to be for them.

When I dropped down the other side,

I had to scramble across people's heads and shoulders.

Some were conscious, some were still alive,

and I were apologising.

I'm saying,

'I'm sorry, I'm sorry

I'm coming in to help you.'

She was lying backwards

Like Jesus on the cross.

Outstretched

Like Jesus on the cross.

Fans were dragging billboards

To try and put bodies on.

The Liverpool fans were the ones trying to assist the injured people

Their priority was to get the fans onto the billboards and they were carrying them across the pitch.

There was just a mass of Liverpool fans doing the same thing.

My first thought was to try to help them,

We kicked down an advertising board.

We kicked it down and a police officer came over and tried to stop us.

He said we'd be arrested.

It was like a battlefield

I remember a policewoman.

She was sitting down, crying.

The whole thing was totally disorganised.

Total chaos.

You didn't know who to grab because there was people everywhere.

Police officers in the pens were getting on with it

I was pulled from behind by a senior officer.

I explained that I was a police officer and was trying to help,

and basically he told me to

Fuck off.

I didn't know how to do the kiss of life

You were just trying to do something instinctively.

Just what I'd seen on the television.

I was in the Air Force before I was in the police

Maybe that's something to do with identifying or having ID tags.

So what was in my mind was that anybody who was walking around wouldn't just come across a relative .

As I tore his shirt open, his wallet came out.

I put it on him so that he could be identified.

I put his shirt over his face.

I just thought it was the right thing to do.

Thinking about this now,

this may have looked like I was looting the dead.

And one of the things that's compounded all this is the reporting in the Sun.

It's always troubled me.

I had maybe photographers photographing me or something,

and it's one thing that's troubled me.

3.14pm

I just wanted to go to sleep.

I was trying to walk away from the Leppings Lane and I kept collapsing.

I could see a line of police officers in the middle of the pitch.

I thought if I walk towards them it will be safe

because it was away from what was going in there

but I kept collapsing.

I collapsed in front of that line.

I remember laying there for ages

and ages.

I couldn't move.

I just wanted to go to sleep.

3.16pm

44 ambulances.

33 being from South Yorkshire and

11 from neighbouring ambulance services.

44 deployed to the disaster,

And three of them got onto the pitch.

Underneath the stands there was two little rooms

I ended up in a gym-type thing.

I just wanted to find my way out.

And I thought,

'Oh this isn't the way out.

I have found myself in a gym.'

There was people everywhere.

Bodies.

People had just been dumped.

One person was still on a board.

It was just chaos in there.

A St John Ambulance volunteer.

A young lass, 14 or 15, longish blonde hair.

She was crying.

She was completely overwhelmed.

She was a kid.

I actually said to her,

'You're a kid.

You should not be seeing this.'

She was left to her own devices,

this kid.

She was just trying to do what she could for people.

she was still trying to help people and she was crying,

she was trying to help people,

even though she was in shock,

out of her depth.

I just put my arm round her and said,

'You're a kid.

You should not be seeing this.'

What sticks in my memory is a group of people

Young men of my own age

wearing replica shirts pulled over their faces to hide their faces.

I can't recall whether those bodies were laying

side by side

or whether it was the situation that there was

one body on top of another.

A youth called over and said, pointing at the pile of all of the Bodies,

'Look at him. I don't know if he's dead.

I don't think he is.'

I looked at the body and saw that he had stopped breathing.

I was of the opinion that he was dead.

However, together with another police officer,

I performed the kiss of life.

I checked the body and believe I felt a pulse.

I remained with the body, which seemed to go into some sort of spasm.

After a time

I have no idea how long

a doctor ran over and looked at the youth, saying,

'He's doing all right'

4.06pm

He was brought to me.

He was on a broken down billboard

Supported by two other football fans.

'Is there anything you can do for this boy?'

He was laid there and this police officer looked at me and he went, 'Oh, he's had it.'

I remember looking down and I thought,

'Oh, my God, it's a little boy.'

The first thing I did was to try and feel a pulse in his wrist.

The pulse that I found was very, very feeble, but it was still there.

It was still there.

We made our way up the slope and into the gymnasium.

We were just told, if they were dead, injured or badly injured, to take them there.

The two police officers who were with me said I'd actually done too much.

I was to stay there with body 51.

I thought it would be best to give some sort of resuscitation
I got down on my hands and knees and proceeded to give
mouth-to-mouth resuscitation.

I thought heart massage may have helped, and I did the worst thing ever.

I actually picked him up which you're not supposed to, because he could have had a neck injury of any sort.

I tried a second time, that's to say I picked him up.

I actually cradled him and I thought,

'You're not going to die. You can't die.'

I remember holding him and I thought, no, he's only a baby.

It can't be happening.

I had his head in my arms and so much of his back,

and that's when his eyes opened and he said, 'Mum'

He looked straight through me.

Then his eyes closed and he just went very, very limp altogether,

So I placed him down on the ground and tried to give him mouth-to-mouth again and heart massage,.

That's when I felt a tap on my shoulder and it was another police officer

and he said, 'Leave him. He's gone. There's nothing you can do.'

4.15pm

A gentleman began to shout into the back garden

It wasn't in the days when we had mobile phones.

He asked us if we could telephone his mum and let her know that he was okay.

He was very pale, very upset.

I said, 'Of course you can, of course you can'

After that, there was a succession of people with phone numbers, which we rang.

We parked the car half a mile from the ground

So I walked back up the tunnel, through the gates

And made my way back to where we parked the car.

We always had a rule,

if we ever got separated,

we'd meet back at the car.

 When I was approaching the car park

I could see that our car was the only car left.

There was no signs of my family.

However, I still went to the car park and I stood there.

The
Evening

We arrived at the Boys' Club

It was just packed, you literally had to push your way through.

I can't remember getting a seat in there.

It was absolute mayhem.

The noise was incredible.

People shouting out.

Just people shouting out names.

'Is such a name on a list?'

The noise was wild.

You couldn't take nothing in.

Nobody approached us.

No police officers came over, there was no communication.

It was just chaos in there, complete chaos.

The only person who came over to us was a resident who offered me a cup of tea.

It was so, so cold in that room.

I was shaking.

This resident came over.

I think she was concerned about me because I was shaking from head to toe, and she offered me a cup of tea, which I couldn't hold because I was shaking so much.

She went and got me a sleeping bag

and I remember I was sat in this sleeping bag and I was trying to keep warm,

and I'd got my arm linked through my mum's and my mum just didn't say a word,

just didn't say one single word.

Every so often they'd stand up and they'd just go,

'Does anybody recognise this jumper?'

'Does anybody recognise these trainers?'

My mum just kept her head down,

'I can't look, I can't look',

Because I think we were so afraid that she was going to see either my brother's jumper –

because we knew what he was wearing that day –

or his trainers.

Because his clothes were his pride and joy.

I remember being in this room with all these strangers

I'm witnessing these people collapsing,

so traumatised at what they've just been told and what they've justfound out,

and then, all of a sudden, to my right there was just this massive scuffle

The media had got in.

They were trying to take photos of us families.

You know, there we are so traumatised,

we don't know what's happening,

we are trying to find out what's happening to our loved ones

and the media have got in

trying to take photographs of us.

The main gymnasium hall

The whole place smelt of school dinners.

It had been a police feeding station prior to the disaster.

And I can't get out of my mind the smell of school dinners.

They were basically brought out in body bags.

Unzipped.

I went to hold his hand and kiss his forehead,

 and we were told not to touch him

 He belonged to the coroner.

I said I was there when he was brought into the world

and I wanted to be there when he was going out of the world.

But the police officer pulled me up roughly and said,

'Sorry, he's the property of the coroner now.

You can't touch him.'

He was wheeled out on a trolley

One of those low ones,

about 16 inches off the ground.

His feet were sticking out.

One was a bare foot and one had a trainer on.

But I know he was very proud of the trainers he'd bought the week before,

so I knew without seeing the face.

I wanted to ring my mother

When the shroud was pulled back,

Again, I asked,

'Can I ring my mother up?'

There was some questions to be asked first.

The very first question asked was what had I had to drink today.

Then I was asked what he had been drinking

what time we got to the ground,

did we have tickets,

what time did we get in.

I didn't think it was appropriate to ask about alcohol.

I was shaking.

I was anxious.

I was crying.

I think there were two police officers

They started asking questions.

The first one was,

'What time did you leave Liverpool?'

The second one,

'What time did you arrive in Sheffield?'

the third,

'Did you go to any pubs on the way before the match?'

and the fourth was,

'How much had you had to drink?'

They asked me that, and even my dad that.

My dad only came to pick us up from Barnsley Hospital.

All they were concerned about was how much alcohol we'd had to drink.

I said, 'I don't know.

We wouldn't have had more than two, two and a half pints',

Because that's all we ever did. And he said,

'Oh, come on, love, they must have had more than that, don't put that past me.'

And he thrust this plastic bag with these two tickets in front of
me,

and he never let go of the bag,

he just leaned across the table, and he said,

'Are these their tickets?

How did they obtain them?

Did they buy them on the black market?

How much would they have paid for them?'

And he was just firing all these questions at me,

he just did not believe anything we said.

He just kept going on and on and on

and I got so upset in the end I just broke down

After

Norman Bettison

I wasn't sure whether he was inspector or chief inspector.

He was on the course.

We would occasionally exchange greetings, words over coffee.

We'd go to the pub afterwards and have one pint. We went most Mondays.

I went into the pub, and Norm Bettison and I got to the bar pretty much simultaneously.

It was just myself and Norman. And Norman said,

'I've been asked by my senior officers to pull together the South Yorkshire Police evidence for the inquiry

and we're going to try and concoct a story that all of the Liverpool fans were drunk

and that we were afraid they were going to break down the gates so we decided to open them.'

I was stunned. I was just staggered. I was shocked.

It was a very matter-of-fact tone.

He was just relating what he'd been told to do.

I got the impression that he saw it as a positive career advancement.

The West Midlands Police came and took a statement

There was one particular feature of this day that they were rather keen on talking about

Alcohol.

That was one of the questions I was asked,

about the amount of alcohol I'd drunk.

And if anybody else was drunk.

That is something they were particularly keen on asking

They didn't ask me how I were, or owt like that.

The first thing

How much had I had to drink?

did I have a ticket to get in the ground;

did I see this?

was there any fighting?

did I see anybody drunk?

have I got a ticket?

Can we have your ticket?

We want to confiscate…

Bombarding me with questions.

Had I got a ticket?

did I have owt to drink?

did I see any fighting?

did I see anybody drunk?

Had I got a ticket?

did I have owt to drink?

did I see any fighting?

did I see anybody drunk?

Had I got a ticket?

did I have owt to drink?

did I see any fighting?

did I see anybody drunk?

Chief Superintendent David Duckenfield decides to tell the truth

Everybody knew the truth.

I said something in the order of,

'Some fans have got in through a gate',

What I didn't say

I didn't say,

'I have authorised the opening of the gates'

I made a dreadful mistake, not realising the consequences of what I was doing,

not telling Mr Kelly that the gates had been opened by me

and that may have contributed to the disaster.

What I would like to say to the Liverpool families is this:

I regret that omission,

and I shall regret it to my dying day.

I had heaped upon them further damage when they had got problems enough.

It was a major mistake on my part.

I have no excuses.
That was a terrible lie,

The fans knew the truth,

that we'd opened the gates;

the police officers knew we'd opened the gates.

With hindsight, I would say I wasn't the best man for the job on the day.

It was a serious mistake.

However, I was the chief superintendent in charge on the day.

So I must accept

responsibility.

The 96

This has been the hardest thing I have ever had to write.

When he was placed on my chest the moment after he was born

I put my arms around this most beautiful, precious child

And a love that I had never experienced before surged out of me for him.

When he died, a part of me also died.

The loss of a child is one of the worst things that can happen to a loving parent.

You lose everything. The present, the future and any purpose.

My pain is centred on what they have missed.

And what our lives would be like now had they not been killed.

We shared so many happy memories.

I remember little things and I find myself laughing.

Now we are left thinking about what he would have achieved:

We will never know, and we are getting older and he will not.

His clothes are still hanging up in his bedroom.

Every so often, mum washes and irons them and hangs them back up.

I thank God that I met him

Loved him and had five beautiful children with him.

Their dad was not a hooligan, but a hardworking family man who just happened to love football.

A man of great integrity who should have been safe when he went to that match that day.

They lived together.

They died together supporting the team they loved.

They only went to watch a game of football.

Hold your head up high

	Age
Jon-Paul Gilhooley	10
Philip Hammond	14
Thomas Anthony Howard	14
Paul Brian Murray	14
Lee Nicol	14
Adam Edward Spearritt	14
Peter Andrew Harrison	15
Victoria Jane Hicks	15
Philip John Steele	15
Kevin Tyrrell	15
Kevin Daniel Williams	15
Kester Roger Marcus Ball	16
Nicholas Michael Hewitt	16
Martin Kevin Traynor	16
Simon Bell	17
Carl Darren Hewitt	17
Keith McGrath	17
Stephen Francis O'Neill	17
Steven Joseph Robinson	17
Henry Charles Rogers	17
Stuart Paul William Thompson	17
Graham John Wright	17
James Gary Aspinall	18
Carl Brown	18
Paul Clark	18
Christopher Barry Devonside	18
Gary Philip Jones	18
Carl David Lewis	18
John McBrien	18
Jonathon Owens	18
Colin Mark Ashcroft	19
Paul William Carlile	19
Gary Christopher Church	19
James Philip Delaney	19

	Age
Sarah Louise Hicks	19
David William Mather	19
Colin Wafer	19
Ian David Whelan	19
Stephen Paul Copoc	20
Ian Thomas Glover	20
Gordon Rodney Horn	20
Paul David Brady	21
Thomas Steven Fox	21
Marian Hazel McCabe	21
Joseph Daniel McCarthy	21
Peter McDonnell	21
Carl William Rimmer	21
Peter Francis Tootle	21
David John Benson	22
David William Birtle	22
Tony Bland	22
Gary Collins	22
Tracey Elizabeth Cox	23
William Roy Pemberton	23
Colin Andrew Hugh William Sefton	23
David Leonard Thomas	23
Peter Andrew Burkett	24
Derrick George Godwin	24
Graham John Roberts	24
David Steven Brown	25
Richard Jones	25
Barry Sidney Bennett	26
Andrew Mark Brookes	26
Paul Anthony Hewitson	26
Paula Ann Smith	26
Christopher James Traynor	26
Barry Glover	27
Gary Harrison	27
Christine Anne Jones	27
Nicholas Peter Joynes	27

	Age
Francis Joseph McAllister	27
Alan McGlone	28
Joseph Clark	29
Christopher Edwards	29
James Robert Hennessy	29
Alan Johnston	29
Anthony Peter Kelly	29
Martin Kenneth Wild	29
Peter Reuben Thompson	30
Stephen Francis Harrison	31
Eric Hankin	33
Vincent Michael Fitzsimmons	34
Roy Harry Hamilton	34
Patrick John Thompson	35
Michael David Kelly	38
Brian Christopher Mathews	38
David George Rimmer	38
Inger Shah	38
David Hawley	39
Thomas Howard	39
Arthur Horrocks	41
Eric George Hughes	42
Henry Thomas Burke	47
Raymond Thomas Chapman	50
John Alfred Anderson	62
Gerard Bernard Patrick Baron	67